ONE

little

VOICE

by
Diane Stelling

illustrated by
Luke, Jonathan, and Thomas Stelling

Published by: Hereami Publishing, P.O. Box 261, Butler,
NJ 07405-0261; (973) 838-2685; Fax: (973) 492-1525.

Library of Congress Catalog Card Number: 97-074836

ISBN 0-9655758-9-6

Printed by The Print Center, NY, NY, USA

This book is dedicated to my Family

Dearest Luke, Jon, and Tom,

May your lives always be as full as these poems. They reflect the good and the bad in people; the joys and frustrations we all experience. Most of all, I want you to remember the fun we had making this book. No matter how young or old you are, you can create beautiful, meaningful things that will touch people, make them think, and maybe even change them. This is a powerful gift. Always remember to use whatever talents you have to build, not to destroy, and to try to have some laughs along the way.

Your most loving

Mom

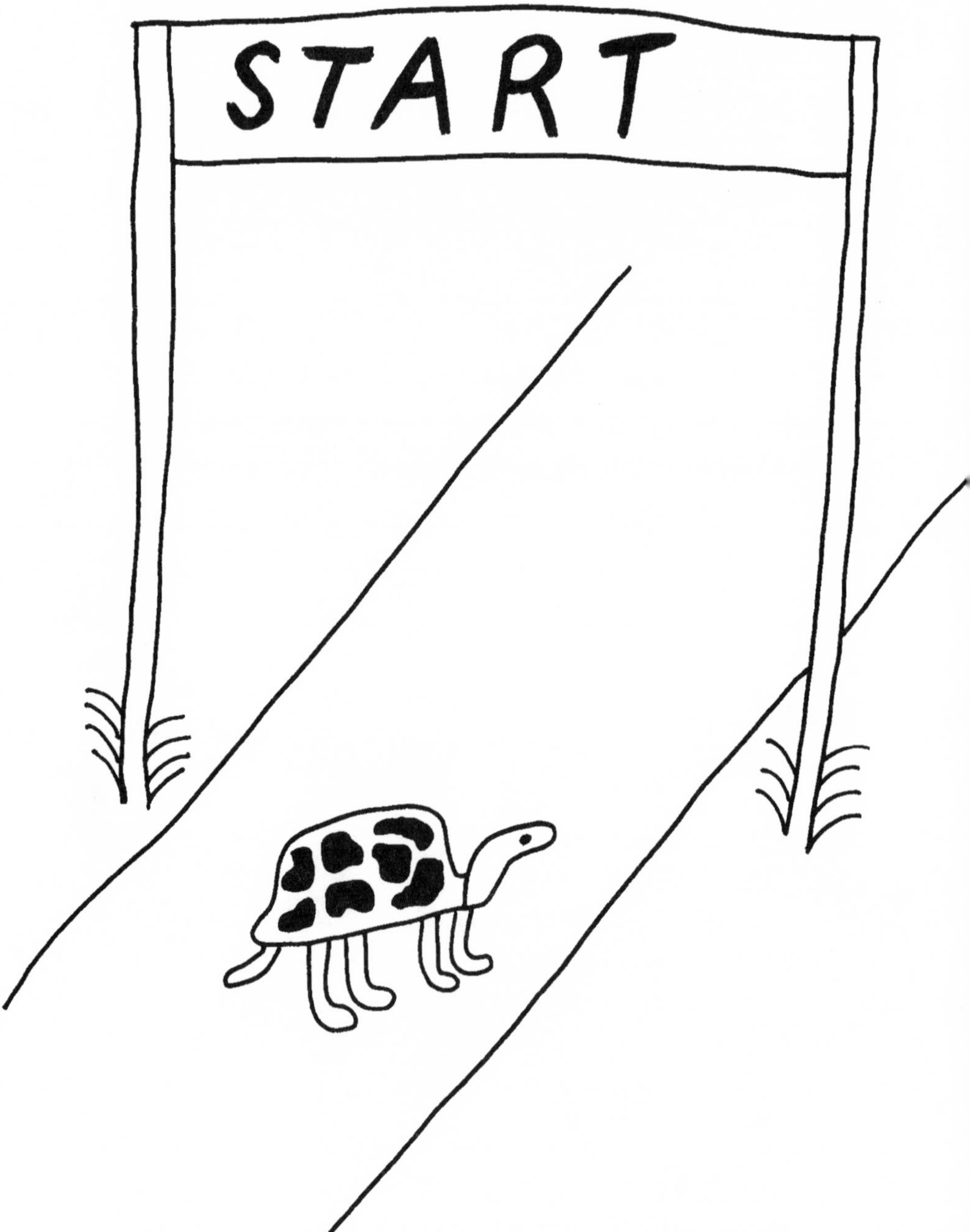
START

THERE'S
ALL
KINDS OF WINNERS

I'm in the race, but I don't know,
Just how it is I got here,
I want to be left all alone,
But it's the same year after year.

Got to be the best and smartest,
Fastest runner in the race,
Can't just sit and watch the others,
Always have to keep the pace.

I don't want to be compared to,
Measured and computerized,
I just want to sit and daydream,
Without being scrutinized.

Everyone says, *"You can do it!"*
"Competition's good for you,"
But remember for each winner,
There must be a loser, too.

Yup, I'm sick of competition,
I've already seen my share,
So if I stay in this darned race,
I'll be the tortoise, not the hare!

SILLY
SALLY
STELLING

Silly Sally Stelling,
    Stalking silently,
Silly Sally Stelling,
    Statuelike, you see.
Silly Sally Stelling,
    Suddenly she springs,
Silly Sally Stelling,
    Surprised suspended string.
Silly Sally Stelling,
    Singing some sweet song,
Silly Sally Stelling,
    Screaming now, so strong.
Silly Sally Stelling,
    Screeching for some supper,
Silly Sally Stelling,
    Shouldn't someone stop her?

Silly Sally Stelling,
    Sitting secretly,
Silly Sally Stelling,
    Stretching stealthily.
Silly Sally Stelling,
    Slipping off the sill,
Silly Sally Stelling,
    Spilled, but stately still.
Silly Sally Stelling,
    Serene and sure she seems,
Silly Sally Stelling,
    Stares straightly as she schemes.
Silly Sally Stelling,
    Spectacular, I say,
Silly Sally Stelling,
    With us she'll surely stay.

ALLWANCE

It's called an allowance,
But I cannot see,
Just exactly what
It allows me.

It's not nearly enough
To buy good stuff,
So I have to decide,
And that's too rough.

If I spend it all quickly,
And buy a small toy,
I'm broke, the toy breaks,
So where is the joy?

If I save up my money,
To get something more,
By the time I can buy it,
I'll be too old, for sure.

I liked it much better,
When I was quite small,
Never worried 'bout money,
Mom and Dad bought it all.

Now my needs are much greater,
The money's too tight,
And I think folks should make
More allowances, right?

WHO TOOK THE
ZIP
OUT OF ZIPPERS?

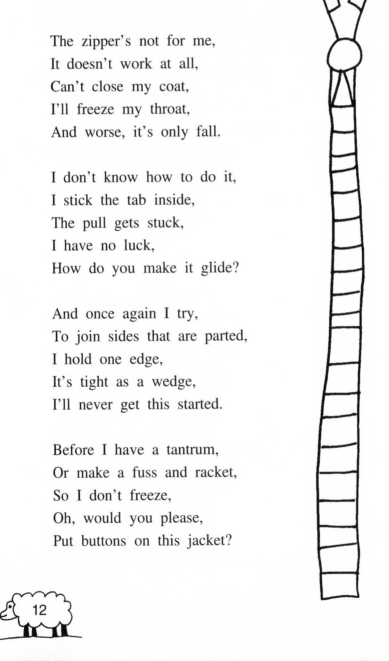

The zipper's not for me,
It doesn't work at all,
Can't close my coat,
I'll freeze my throat,
And worse, it's only fall.

I don't know how to do it,
I stick the tab inside,
The pull gets stuck,
I have no luck,
How do you make it glide?

And once again I try,
To join sides that are parted,
I hold one edge,
It's tight as a wedge,
I'll never get this started.

Before I have a tantrum,
Or make a fuss and racket,
So I don't freeze,
Oh, would you please,
Put buttons on this jacket?

THE BULLY AND ME

"Gimme your snack,"
The bully said to me.
I didn't want to do it,
But then he punched me.

"Gimme your money,"
The bully said to me.
I went to tell the teacher,
But then he threatened me.

"Better not tell,"
The bully said to me,
"I'll beat you up right after school,
And THEN you'll see!"

"Gimme your lunch,"
The bully said to me.
I thought a lot about it,
And got as mad as could be.

So..........

I bopped him one.

13

"GET YOUR SNEAKERS ON!"

Can't find my sneakers,
Don't really care,
Checked every room,
Looked everywhere -

Under the bed
In the toybox
Behind the dresser
On the boot tray
In the hamper
Under the kitchen table
Behind the bathroom door
On the top bunk
Beside the sofa cushions
Out in the garage
In my wastebasket.

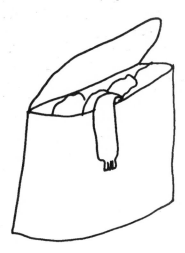

Where'd they go?
Where can they be?
I don't know,
It puzzles me.

Wait - how about
In my closet,
Way back there,
In the bottom,
In the corner,
In the dark - is it?.....
YES!
I found ONE....

SHOWOFF

Mine's the biggest,
And the best,
It is the fastest
In the West.
And the neatest
Ever seen,
The very meanest
Of the mean.
Taller than
The tallest tree,
It is the coolest
That you'll see.
And best of all,
What is most fine,
You can't have it,
It's all mine!

CRABBY CACTUS

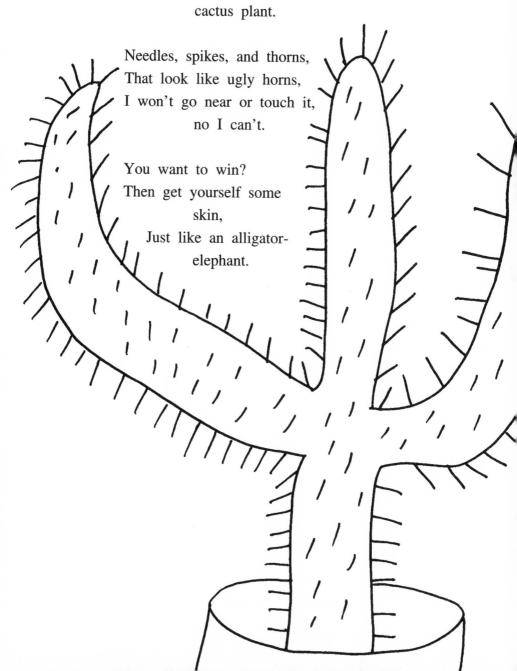

Oochy, ouchy,
It makes me very grouchy,
I don't like this mean old
       cactus plant.

Needles, spikes, and thorns,
That look like ugly horns,
I won't go near or touch it,
       no I can't.

You want to win?
Then get yourself some
       skin,
    Just like an alligator-
       elephant.

COPYCAT

My eyes are on my paper,
I'm looking straight ahead,
But once in awhile I see this kid,
Do something that I dread.

He looks at me and then my desk,
And tries to peek around
My elbow which is on my test,
I see him glare, then frown.

I know he's stuck and doesn't know
The answers that he should,
I guess he didn't study much,
I'd help him if I could.

He nudges me and catches my eye,
And whispers very low,
Why does he have to pick on me?
I wish he wouldn't, you know.

I try my best to ignore this kid,
But he doesn't go away,
Maybe I'll just relax my arm,
He probably can't see, anyway.

I guess that wasn't bad at all,
He got what he was needing,
And I was not involved at all,
In any of the cheating.

What!?
What are we doing back here?
NOTHING!
You want to see
Both of us
And our papers
RIGHT NOW !?!?

DETERMINATION

Have you ever seen a bunch of rocks,
Where it seems like nothing could grow,
And in a crevice, a crooked tree stands,
And you wonder, how can it be so?

Have you ever seen a concrete path,
Its barren surface too clean,
And in the cracks between the blocks,
Lush grass is growing so green.

Have you ever seen a tiny ant,
With a crumb so big he's diminished,
He struggles along back towards his hole,
Never stopping until he's finished.

Have you ever seen a baby crawl,
Pull itself up with all its might,
Then it falls and cries and tries again,
Until it can get it right.

Have you ever thought about these things,
With wonder and admiration,
Why is it that we never give up?
It's simple determination.

IF I'VE HEARD IT ONCE...

"I'm not in the mood for silly shenanigans."
"Learn to quit while you're ahead."
"Why must you be such a wiseguy?"
"Can't you calm it down instead?"
"What's the matter?   What's bothering you?"
"Don't argue with me, just do as I say."
"Can't you see you're driving me crazy?"
"You're quite a motor-mouth today."
"Mind your own business, it's not about you."
"It's your fault, you should have known."
"When are you ever going to grow up?"
"Someday you're going to be on your own."
"I feel like I'm talking to the wall."
"You'll never do it if you don't try."
"What was it that you just mumbled?"
"Because I said so, that's why!"

I'm writing all this down, you see,
And hope I'll never forget,
So when I have kids I'll be quite sure,
Not to say things that I'll regret.

MY FAVORITE FOOD GROUPS

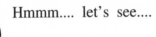

Hmmm.... let's see....

Root Group
Potatoes, carrots, radishes, root beer, and turnips (yuck).

Tree Group
Apples, oranges, bananas, plums, and pears.

Bush Group
Broccoli, corn, green beans, peas, pineapples, tomatoes, and spinach (yuck).

Tall Grass Group
Bread, cereal, rice, and pasghetti.

Nut Group
Walnuts, almonds, cashews, pistachios, peanuts, coconuts, and donuts.

Stuff From Animals Group

Milk, cheese, yogurt, ice cream, butter, and eggs.

Walking Animal Parts Group

Hamburgers, hot dogs, pork chops, bacon, and liver (yuck).

Flying Animal Parts Group

Chicken (including nuggets), turkey, goose, and duck (including peeking).

Swimming Animal Parts Group

Fish fingers, crab, lobster, shrimp, and scallops.

And finally.....

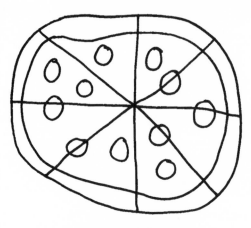

Junk Food Group

Candy bars, pizza, potato chips, pretzels, popcorn, gum, cupcakes, brownies, chocolate chip cookies, lollipops, licorice, chocolate covered raisins and peanuts, jujubes, hard candy, candy apples, caramel covered popcorn and peanuts, cotton candy, cheese puffs, ices, nougat, potato sticks, candy corn, fudge, gum drops, salt water taffy, jelly beans, soda, ice cream, mints, candy canes, truffles, cream-filled cakes, marshmallows, hot fudge sauce, sprinkles, hot cocoa, pudding, frosting, eclairs, and bon bons.

**Yup,
Just as I thought.
Four groups aren't enough.**

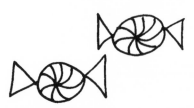

THE UNIVERSAL CHILDHOOD DISEASE

It's an annoying disease,
That grownups don't get,
It affects only kids,
And there's no cure yet.

Attacks always occur,
When you need to be quiet,
In church or assemblies,
Mealtimes are a riot.

It affects everyone,
Boy, I hope I outgrow it,
And learn to control,
When and where I can sit.

It's driving my folks
Mad and crazy for sure,
Understand I can't help it,
So please look out for -

THE FIDGETS!

25

THE STUFF THAT'S ALL OVER THE BATHROOM THAT MOM'S ALWAYS YELLING ABOUT!

I love this stuff,
It's really great,
Let's get some now,
I just can't wait.
It comes in flavors,
Colors and gel,
Stripes and sparkles,
I know them all well.
You can pump it up,
Or squish it out,
So what is all
The fuss about?

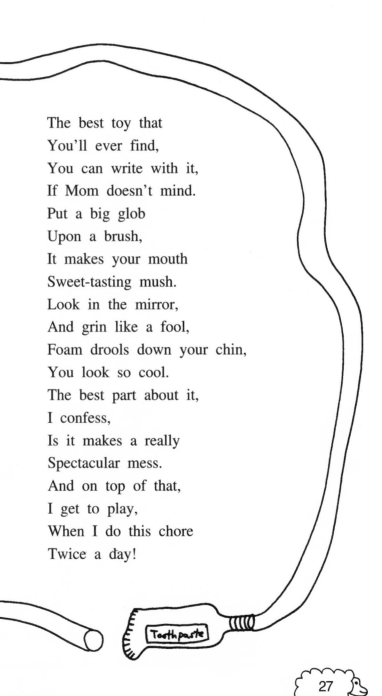

The best toy that
You'll ever find,
You can write with it,
If Mom doesn't mind.
Put a big glob
Upon a brush,
It makes your mouth
Sweet-tasting mush.
Look in the mirror,
And grin like a fool,
Foam drools down your chin,
You look so cool.
The best part about it,
I confess,
Is it makes a really
Spectacular mess.
And on top of that,
I get to play,
When I do this chore
Twice a day!

Toothpaste

WHEN EVERYBODY
WANTS A MOM

When I'm sick and I don't feel good,
I'm a pretty sorry sight,
I want my Mom to stay right with me,
Tell me I will be all right.

She puts her cool hand on my forehead,
Pats my cheek and gives a smile,
Fluffs my pillow, smooths the covers,
Then I drift asleep awhile.

If I wake up with a bad dream,
Sweating, scared, and very warm,
Mom will come and make it better,
She'll hold me, I can't be harmed.

She sits and chats and takes my temp,
My medicine tastes yucky,
She also brings my meals to me,
I guess I'm very lucky.

For when I feel so small and weak,
And want to be secure,
Mom is always there for me,
Of this I can be sure.

And so when Mom gets sick herself,
I know she must feel bad,
Her Mom's not there to comfort her,
It's up to me and Dad.

I know it's not the same for her,
But still I really try,
So when I bring a meal to her,
Why does she smile, then cry?

OUCH

Don't you touch it,
I'm okay,
Leave it there,
For another day.
It only hurts
A little bit,
I'm sure that I'll
Get used to it.
It's gonna hurt,
Don't take it out,
Pain is something
I can do without.
Maybe if
It's left alone,
It'll come right out
All on its own.
It's not too big,
Or very deep,
It's something I
Would like to keep.
I'd like to wait
Until next winter,
For you to remove
This darned old splinter.

MY GRANDMA'S SWEATER

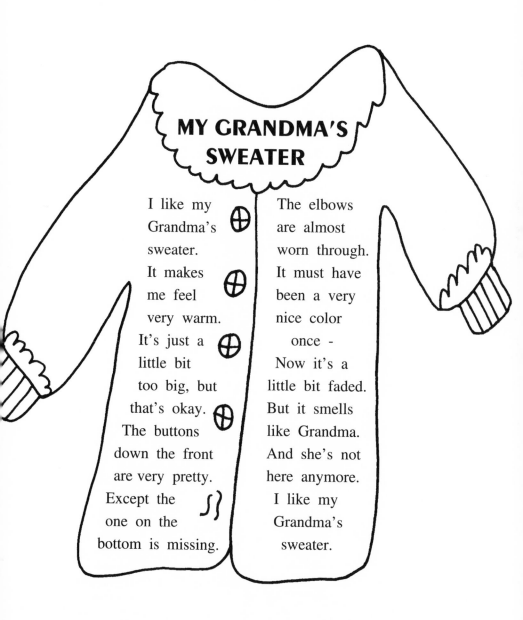

I like my
Grandma's
sweater.
It makes
me feel
very warm.
It's just a
little bit
too big, but
that's okay.
The buttons
down the front
are very pretty.
Except the
one on the
bottom is missing.

The elbows
are almost
worn through.
It must have
been a very
nice color
once -
Now it's a
little bit faded.
But it smells
like Grandma.
And she's not
here anymore.
I like my
Grandma's
sweater.

ONE LITTLE VOICE

Sometimes I feel so bad I think,
Why should I even try?
What's the use? I'm one little voice,
I give up, shrug my shoulders, and sigh.

No one will hear, or care at all,
Or even pay attention,
There are so many other voices out there,
Too numerous to mention.

And then I think, those voices I hear,
Although they speak quite loud,
They say things I don't believe in at all,
But still they attract a crowd.

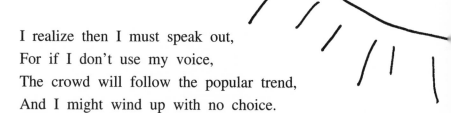

I realize then I must speak out,
For if I don't use my voice,
The crowd will follow the popular trend,
And I might wind up with no choice.

So I speak up and hope that others will hear,
And not find my views too strange,
For if they will join me, believe in my voice,
Only then can we get things to change.

But even if no one pays much attention,
I certainly should rejoice,
Because I have the gift of freedom,
To use my one little voice.

Baa

SUPPLY AND DEMAND

When you get low on hugs and kisses,
You need to go back for more,
They're what you need in great supply,
But they're not in any store.

The nicest thing about them, though,
I'm not really too sure why,
Is when you start to spread them around,
They begin to multiply.

The more you give, the more you get,
They never seem to end,
The love that hugs and kisses bring,
Is something on which to depend.

But most of all, remember this,
For it's no idle boast,
Whenever you want a hug the least,
Is when you need it the most.

HANDICAPPED

My friend can't talk.
He doesn't know how.
There's something wrong with him.
He gets upset when
I don't understand him.
But he's okay.
He always tries hard and
He understands me.
We weren't always friends.
I used to think he was dumb.
I didn't know he had a problem.
It must be hard for him
To go through life.
Not only can't he talk,
But people are annoyed with him.
They don't get the chance
To know him inside.
He's not stupid.
He tries to be like everyone else.
To be accepted.
But his handicap gets in the way.
When I see people being mean to him,
Sometimes I wonder what's really
Getting in the way,
And who has the worse handicap?

BUSY, BUSY, BUSY

I wish the day wouldn't end,
There's so much to play and do,
Someday my folks will understand,
That sleep can wait 'til I'm through.

I need to finish my games,
To read one more funny book,
I have to complete this puzzle tonight,
I'm not tired, just take a look.

Should I go outside and play?
My favorite show's on TV,
The choices are hard, there's not enough time,
As you can all plainly see.

I want my friend to stay longer,
Can I have another snack?
The day went so fast, I had so much fun,
I couldn't even keep track.

And now they want me in bed,
My teeth I have to brush,
I need another glass of water,
They always make me rush.

Someday I'll need to sleep,
When I'm twenty or thirty, perhaps,
But while I'm young with so much to do,
I can just get by with some naps.

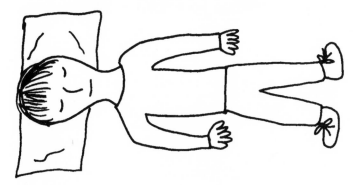

THE BOWLING BLUES SOLUTION

Why is the ball so heavy?
Why are the pins so far away?
Why is the lane so narrow?
Who thought up this game anyway?
Why do they have those gutters?
Where else can the darn ball go?
Who can get it down the alley?
When you aim it straight, it goes too slow.
Why do you wear such funny shoes?
Who can figure out the score?
Why is the lane so slippery?
Want to hear anymore?
The only way I like this game,
The only way I hit some pins,
Is when they fill the gutters up
With bumpers, then I surely win.
There's just one problem I can see,
Tho' bumpers are so cool,
The ball zigzags so much that it
Feels like I'm playing pool.

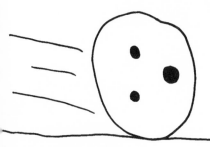

IT'S ALL IN
YOUR ATTITUDE

What is an attitude?
*It is the clothing
That our feelings
And faces wear.*

REVENGE
OF THE
WATER FOUNTAIN

High ones, low ones,
Big and overgrown ones,
All I want to do is get a drink.

Push the button, turn the knob,
Stomp the pedal, what a job,
All I want to do is get a drink.

It seems so near, and yet so far,
'Cause I'm too short to reach it, **grr....**
All I want to do is get a drink.

If I get a kindly boost,
Then I must precariously roost,
All I want to do is get a drink.

Turn the knob, check the spout,
Water dribbles slowly out,
All I want to do is get a drink.

Turn it more, just like a hose,
Oops! Water gushes up my nose,
Why won't it ever let me get a drink?!

LETHAL WEAPONS

They tell me that
Sticks and stones
Can break my bones,
But names can never harm me.

They're wrong.

Sometimes people say things
That are so mean,
The words stay in my head
Long after my body heals.

They hurt me deeply.

And the more I believe
The words are true,
The longer they stay
And give me pain.

Like an invisible wound.

So be careful what you say.
You may not know when
You are hurting someone inside
Beyond repair.

TATTLE TALE

She hit me,
He bit me,
Do you know what **he** did?

He's yelling,
She's telling,
Do you know what **she** did?

She thinks she's right,
They're in a fight,
Do you know what **they** did?

They're not working,
He keeps smirking,
Do you know what **he** did?

He's not walking,
She's always talking,
Do you know what **she** did?

She's pushing,
They're rushing,
Do you know what *they* did?

They won't eat lunch,
He gave me a punch,
Do you know what *he* did?

He changed places,
She's making faces,
Do you know what *she* did?

They always tease,
Oh help me, please,
Do you know what *they* did?

And what did *I* do?

Oh, nothing.....

THE LAW OF GRAVITY

Floors are tricky,
Sidewalks, too,
When you're not looking,
They smack into you.

You can walk along,
Pick up the pace,
And before you know it,
They're right in your face.

I'm always surprised,
It's not like I slip,
Nothing's in the way,
Over which I can trip.

But I'm drawn like a magnet,
This mystery confounds,
So until it is solved,
Keep your eyes on the ground.

44

TOON IN

What do I like to do best in the world?
What really appeals to me?
Why that is the easiest question of all,
Watching Saturday morning TV!

Every channel you watch, all morning long,
Has cartoons and puppet shows,
The hosts are all silly, it's so much fun,
As every kid surely knows.

The commercials are great, they sell such neat stuff,
All the toys that I'd like to buy,
The candy and cereals look good to me,
I'd like to give them a try.

And the best thing of all, there is no school,
I get to watch in pjs,
Mom and Dad don't complain, they're asleep in their room,
I can sit and be silly all day.

I'd like to see a new law created,
I'm serious, don't get me wrong,
Why can't Saturday morning TV,
Last the entire week long?

45

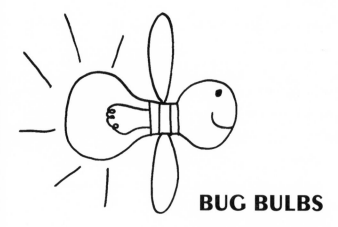

BUG BULBS

Lightning bugs, oh lightning bugs,
Like stars amongst the grass,
Twinkling through the dusky eve,
How did you come to pass?

A light bulb on a little bug,
Is such a neat idea,
But as I frolic with you,
For your safety I do fear.

As you light the night before me,
Like a city from afar,
Please learn to fly much faster or
You'll wind up in a jar!

WHERE IS GOD?

I've never seen God.
They tell me He's here, but I wonder....

If He is here,
Why do we have wars, and
Hunger, and homeless people, and
Sickness, and killing, and stealing?

I wish the world was a perfect place,
Full of only beautiful sunsets, and
Gorgeous flowers, and breathtaking mountains, and
Tropical fish, and gentle people, and unending love.

The world is full of all these things,
The bad and the good.

And when I see the good, I think,
"That is what God intended the world to be."
And when I see the bad, I think,
"That is why we still need Him so much."

And maybe, just maybe,
If more and more people
Carried a little bit of God inside themselves,
The bad things would wither away.

So perhaps I've been searching too hard for Him.
I need only to look in my heart.

MISNAMED

I wonder why
It's a butterfly,
It would make much more sense
As a flutterby.

And what is with
The hummingbirds?
Can't they sing?
Forgot the words?

And what about
The old palm tree?
Can your palm fit around it?
Seems strange to me.

And when you don't eat,
They call it a fast,
But you drink very slow,
To make it last.

And the pussywillow
Is missing the cat,
An animal bush,
Who thought of that?

And if a galosh
Is an overshoe,
Shouldn't a sock
Be an overfoot, too?

And a belly button
Is really weird,
Suppose it pops open?
I've always feared.

And the babysitter
Doesn't sit,
Nor am I a baby,
Let's get rid of it.

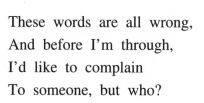

And the dandelion
Is dandy, I know,
But it's not a lion,
It's crazy, no?

These words are all wrong,
And before I'm through,
I'd like to complain
To someone, but who?

49

CHAIR DARE

Beware,
Mr. Chair.
You have a flair,
For catching hair,
And underwear.
So I dare
You to be fair,
Try not to tear,
Or even snare,
But always spare,
What we wear.
Please take care.
So there!

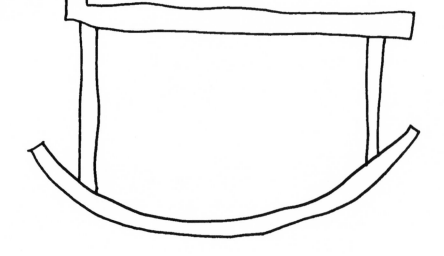

TELL ME

Cats purr and meow,
      But how?
How do birds fly?
      And why?
Why's a horse need a shoe?
      And from who?
Who's first, egg or hen?
      And when?
When porcupines care,
      They kiss....where?
Where's the answers? Do not
      Just say, *"WHAT?"*

A TIMELY PROBLEM

What time is it? What time is it?
This really should be easy,
But telling time can sometimes make
A person rather queasy.

The little hand, it tells the hour,
With this I have no fear,
But the minutes I can't understand,
It certainly isn't clear.

It's not a "1," but "5 minutes after,"
The "2" becomes a "10,"
The "3" is quarter past the hour,
I'm really confused then.

It only gets worse as we go along,
Half past the hour is next,
Instead of "after" we have "before,"
This clock is truly hexed.

How can "after the hour" come before "before"?
Or "until" come after "past"?
It's so confusing I just give up,
But there is some help at last.

Some folks out there, like me, I guess,
Whose invention I will not mock,
Helped me out tremendously,
By creating the digital clock!

SPECIALS ARE SPECIAL

I like my special subjects,
Like Music and Art and Gym,
They get me away from all the other
Boring subjects I'm in.

Music's fun, we listen and sing,
Make motions, move, and sway,
I wish that Social Studies could
Be taught to us this way.

The projects are so great in Art,
With messes I wouldn't miss,
All glitter, markers, paint, and clay,
Why can't Math class be like this?

And Gym's the best, we run around,
Play games and scream and shout,
I always thought that is what
Language class should be about.

But it's no use, for it won't change,
So I'm thankful, to be sure,
I've got my specials to get me through,
Other subjects I can't endure.

54

MARKER

FREEDOM

The opportunity
To disagree,
To be whatever
I want to be,
To see whatever
There is to see,
Without someone
Always watching me,
That's what it means
To really be free.

WHAT IS IT?

Green, brown, orange, yellow,
The tastes are all the same,
I can't tell what it is, and yet
It's lunch, this is a shame.

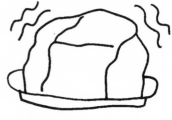

Green, brown, orange, yellow,
It's mystery meat today,
The veggie looks and smells to me,
Like lima beans puree.

Green, brown, orange, yellow,
Dumped with a giant spoon,
They nuked this food, it's soggy,
And they took it out too soon.

Green, brown, orange, yellow,
Potatoes just like paste,
And as they cool they get rock hard,
Good Lord, it's such a waste.

Green, brown, orange, yellow,
It bounces and it wiggles,
Doesn't matter what it is,
Can't eat it without giggles.

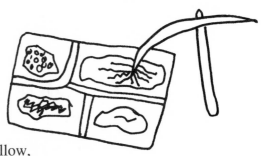

Green, brown, orange, yellow,
It must have been one day,
Real food before they killed it all,
And put it on my tray.

> Green, brown, orange, yellow,
> I'm not sure I'll survive,
> I need a plan to get me through
> School lunch and stay alive.

> Green, brown, orange, yellow,
> One of the safest tips,
> Is only eat the packaged food,
> Like ice cream and the chips.

Green, brown, orange, yellow,
This isn't good for me,
I want nutrition, but this food's
INEDIBLE, you see?!?!

Green, brown, orange, yellow,
Can't solve this with a poem,
The only solution I can see,
Is to bring my lunch from home!

HOW
SHOULD
I
BE?

What is wrong with me?
I hope I grow up soon,
'Cause everything I say or do,
Somehow I completely ruin.

I always say things wrong,
Stick my foot in my mouth,
The only hope I have so far,
Is people blame my youth.

I never know how to act,
I'm clumsy, like a fool,
I bump and spill and hit and trip,
I guess I'm not "Mr. Cool."

The harder that I try,
The more I seem to miss,
The biggest fear I have is that
I'll always be like this.

58

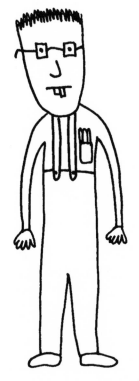

Maybe I shouldn't fret,
It's not as bad as it seems,
If only my confidence would grow,
It would give me self-esteem.

And then I'd be the best,
So cool and hip and free,
The only trouble with it is,
That really isn't me.

So maybe I'm just stuck,
It's really what was meant,
If I could just get used to me,
I'd finally be content.

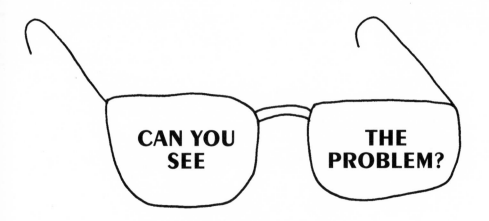

CAN YOU SEE THE PROBLEM?

How are things supposed to look?
Is it all just in my mind?
Lately I've been thinking that
Perhaps I'm going blind.

Sometimes things look all fuzzy,
'Stead of one thing I see two,
Maybe I'm just growing up,
Does it look like this to you?

I learned to read and it was great,
But only for a while,
For now it's all a blur to me,
Like when my teacher smiles.

No one told me this would happen,
Guess I should get used to it,
Bet my parents went through this, too,
So I'll keep it my secret.

NOTHING
BUT A BAD HABIT

Just because I'm a
    nail-biting,
    thumb-sucking,
    skin-picking,
    knuckle-cracking,
    hair-twisting,
    nose-picking,
    foot-jiggling,
    big, burping mess
Doesn't mean you can't love me.
Anyway, I'm going to stop..........

tomorrow.

WHICH SPORT'S FOR
YOU?

There's baseball and football,
And volleyball, too,
Basketball, wrestling,
To name just a few.

Jai alai and kayaking,
Fencing and tennis,
Those guys who play hockey,
Can be quite a menace.

Don't forget soccer,
Badminton, lacrosse,
The regal equestrian,
Riding their horse.

From England we have
Many sports like croquet,
Polo, cricket and rugby,
To round out the day.

How 'bout running and surfing,
And rodeo stuff,
Paint ball and laser tag,
Aren't too tough.

Bullfighting is dangerous,
But who is to blame?
Racquet and handball,
And squash are more tame.

Skeet-shooting and riflery,
Both need reloads,
Dirt-biking and sledding,
Are way off the roads.

Swimming, gymnastics,
And skating galore,
Both roller and ice,
And blading, and more.

Track is both running,
    And jumping, it's neat,
        But hang-gliding relies
            On some wings, not on feet.

    For those with a death wish,
        There is bungee jumping,
            As well as sky diving,
                They're both really something.

There's archery, hunting,
And boxing and darts,
Sheer mountain climbing,
Tough martial arts.

Then.....

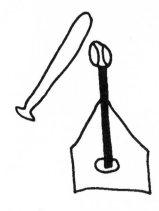

Horse racing, weightlifting,
Curling on ice,
Shuffleboard, bowling,
And marbles are nice.

Tossing the caber,
Is such a strong feat,
Bobsledding and sumo,
Are also quite neat.

To round out the field sports,
Let's try to name all,
There's kick, dodge, and soft,
As well as T-ball.

You can bicycle, jog,
Or try to catch fish,
Maybe go for a hike,
Even sail, if you wish.

Snorkeling, boat racing,
Scuba, high diving,
Like bocce and horseshoes,
Are certainly thriving.

Golf is real calm,
And very rewarding,
For ultimate thrills,
We have skate and snow boarding.

Shot put and javelin,
Need a sure hand,
How 'bout skiing as well on both
Water and land.

Cheerleading and twirling,
Pole vaulting and pool,
Dog sled and car racing,
Are all very cool.

For the non-claustrophobic,
There's caving, you know,
It's known as spelunking,
Exploring below.

Acrobatics and rowing,
Canoeing and such,
Frisbee and ping-pong,
They are a bit much.

Despite all of these,
It's so plain to me,
The most favorite

sport,

Is **watching TV!**

AN INTERESTING IDEA

What is an idea?
It is a road map
Your brain uses
To get from a problem
To a solution.

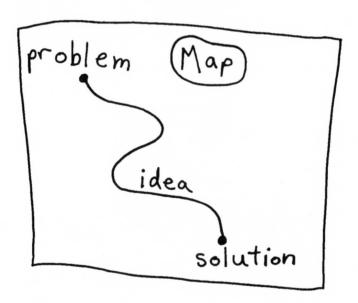

NOBODY'S PERFECT

Why do you always have to go first?
Why can't I be first this one time?
And why do you always have to be right?
Being wrong is not such a crime.

Why must you always have the last word?
Why won't you listen to me?
Why do we have to do things *your* way?
This isn't fair, can't you see?

Nobody's perfect, I know that is true,
So why must you always be best?
Why won't you step aside for a change?
Let someone else take care of the rest.

Don't think you've won, I'm not giving up,
Although you're stubborn and proud,
Because even if you are bigger than me,
I can yell twice as loud!

THE MOVING BLUES

Why do they have to move?
Why do they have to go?
Why can't they stay and play forever?
Please say it isn't so.

When are they going to move?
When will we see them again?
When are they going to come back and visit?
I'll just sit and mope until then.

Who will move into their house?
Who will be friends with me now?
Who will I visit and play with each day?
I don't want new friends anyhow.

Why do I feel so bad?
Why is it so unfair?
Why is everyone smiling and happy?
I'll miss them so much, I don't care.

It's not easy to move away,
There's so much you have on your mind,
Even though it's exciting, adventurous too,
It's hard on the folks left behind.

No matter how bad I might feel,
Though I've lost a very good friend,
I feel for my friend who is leaving us all,
And who has to start over again.

THE JUNE DRAWER

I brought it into school with me,
Didn't play with it for long,
Put it in my desk for later,
Why was that so very wrong?

I didn't let it interefere,
With work I had to do,
I only played when I was bored,
The lessons really flew.

The other kids all liked my toy,
And thought that it was cool,
No one ever told me not
To play with it in school.

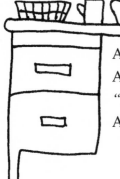

And so my teacher took my toy
Away and cried, *"No more!"*
"You'll get it back in June," she said,
And stuck it in her drawer.

I've lost it now, it's gone forever,
I know she won't remember,
'Cause June is such a long way off,
Right now it's only September!

RULES FOR LIFE

Don't say can't.
Never say never.
Nothing's impossible,
Love is forever.

SWIMMING LESSON

It's way too deep,
And way too cold,
I'll stand right here,
Until I'm old.
Please don't let go,
I know I'll sink,
I'm not a fish,
I'm scared, I think.
Let someone else,
Please take my place,
I don't like water,
In my face.
I'll hold my breath,
Until I'm dead,
But I won't ever,
Dunk my head.

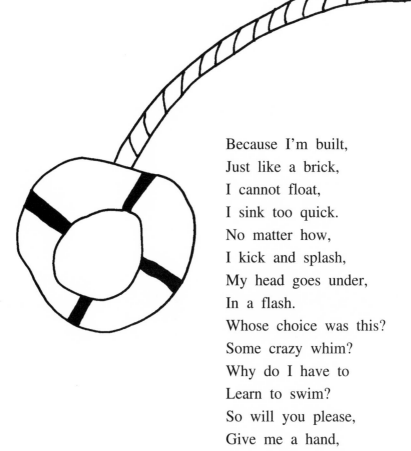

Because I'm built,
Just like a brick,
I cannot float,
I sink too quick.
No matter how,
I kick and splash,
My head goes under,
In a flash.
Whose choice was this?
Some crazy whim?
Why do I have to
Learn to swim?
So will you please,
Give me a hand,
So I can get,
To dry, hard land?!

MIRRORVISION

It's better than a camera,
It's better than TV,
I call it mirrorvision,
It's lots of fun for me.

The best part of it is,
I dress up and pretend,
And make the silliest faces,
Along with my mirror friend.

No matter how I act,
My friend just lets me be,
And follows everything I do,
My mirror friend and me.

LOST

They're lost again, lost again, hopelessly lost,
Why do they do this to me?
They were both here just a minute ago,
I wonder where they can be?

We all came together, it started out fine,
Oh, what a beautiful day,
But I turned my head, and they disappeared,
Why did they wander away?

We talked about it before we left home,
We said we'd stick close by each other,
Why don't they ever listen to me?
I've lost them for sure, oh brother....

The day is now ruined, I'll never get home,
It's the worst day I've ever had,
Please somebody help me, I need to find out,
What happened to Mom and Dad?

FLOWERY CONVERSATION

Hya, Cinth!
These flowers are for Sythia.
And Jon Quil's tu lips say he'll play,
With Mums or chids there with ya!

SUMMER VACATION

Summer, summer, what a bummer,
No more schoolwork left to do,
Projects, quizzes, time just whizzes,
It's all over, guess I'm through.

Social studies, science buddies,
Where will all my friends go now?
Horsing around, in the playground,
No more fighting, holy cow!

Mathematics, acrobatics,
Standardized tests were too few,
Those spelling bees were such a breeze,
Nothing to look forward to.

Teachers nagging, grades all sagging,
Homework piled to the sky,
Sitting quiet, what a riot,
I'll be sad to say good-bye...

(Fooled ya, didn't I?)

77

WHY DO PEOPLE DO IT?

They tell me that it's bad,
But it is all around,
It is the ugliest habit,
That I have ever found.

Adults say, *"Don't do it,"*
But their words never fit,
For they give a little speech,
And then THEY go and do it.

"You can't stop it once you start,"
Is the excuse they use,
"Don't wind up stuck like me,
Or you will surely lose."

I'll never be like them,
Because I'm not a fool,
Although my friends and all the ads,
Say that I'll be cool.

It's expensive and dirty,
It'll kill you.....that's no joke,
So with all this information,
Why do people smoke?

WHAT'S WITH THIS WORD, ANYWAY?

There's a word right in our language,
That will always cause a smile,
It has no class or grace or couth,
But gosh, it's got tremendous style.

Don't know what there is about it,
Why it causes so much glee,
How can one word make a difference?
This one really puzzles me.

It's a fact this word's so silly,
Laughter I would never begrudge,
But people should have self-control,
Wait - I will let you be the judge.

Are you ready? Want to try it?
First we have to set the scene,
Make yourself all calm and serious,
Now you'll see just what I mean -

BOOGERS!

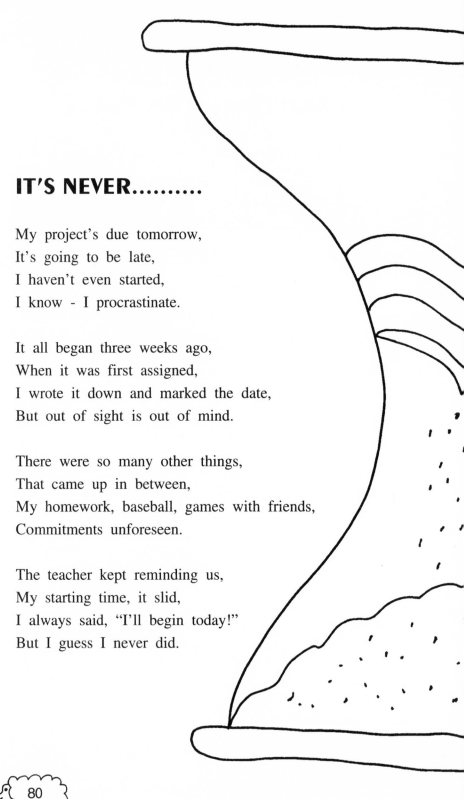

IT'S NEVER.........

My project's due tomorrow,
It's going to be late,
I haven't even started,
I know - I procrastinate.

It all began three weeks ago,
When it was first assigned,
I wrote it down and marked the date,
But out of sight is out of mind.

There were so many other things,
That came up in between,
My homework, baseball, games with friends,
Commitments unforeseen.

The teacher kept reminding us,
My starting time, it slid,
I always said, "I'll begin today!"
But I guess I never did.

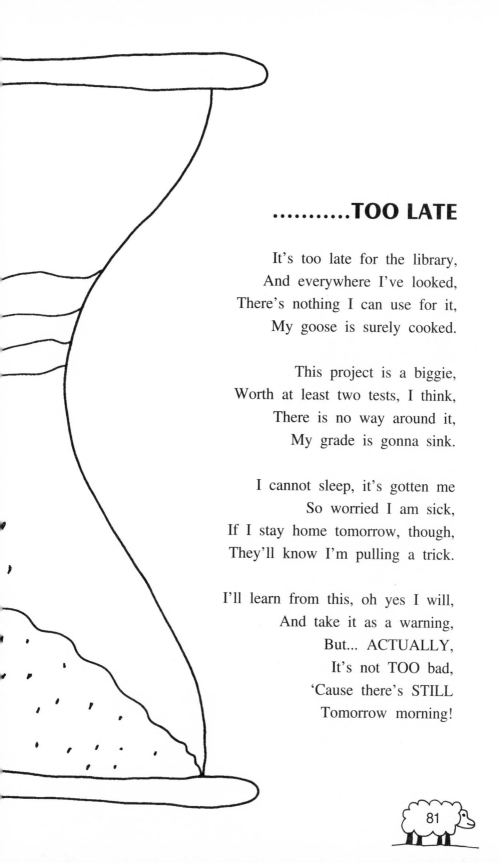

..........TOO LATE

It's too late for the library,
And everywhere I've looked,
There's nothing I can use for it,
My goose is surely cooked.

This project is a biggie,
Worth at least two tests, I think,
There is no way around it,
My grade is gonna sink.

I cannot sleep, it's gotten me
So worried I am sick,
If I stay home tomorrow, though,
They'll know I'm pulling a trick.

I'll learn from this, oh yes I will,
And take it as a warning,
But... ACTUALLY,
It's not TOO bad,
'Cause there's STILL
Tomorrow morning!

SUCCESS

People always talk about,
This thing they call success,
They spend their lives all chasing it,
Won't settle for anything less.

Perhaps I'll be a movie star,
Or play pro basketball,
Gosh, maybe I'll join a punk rock band,
And then I'll have it all.

More money than I'll ever need,
Fans far as you can see,
No one will tell me what to do,
They'll all wait and listen to me.

I'll run a corporation,
Make deals all day and night,
Hire and fire, buy and sell,
Until I get it right.

More money than I'll ever need,
Employees as far as you can see,
No one will tell me what to do,
They'll all wait and listen to me.

Is money, fame, and power success?
Most people tell me so,
But folks I know don't have these things,
Yet they're successful, this I know.

It doesn't matter what they do,
Or how much school they've had,
It's how they treat each other,
That makes it good or bad.

They do their best, whatever it is,
Find time to tease and chat,
They relate to folks, and feelings, and stuff,
Their happiness comes from that.

So to be successful, I believe,
It's most important, by far,
To really care about other people,
And accept them the way they are.

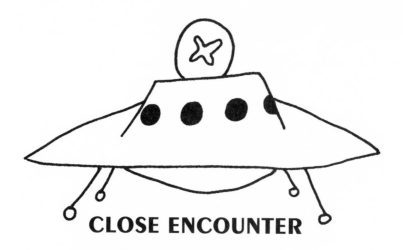

CLOSE ENCOUNTER

What would I do if an alien
Came into my room at night?
With his UFO parked on my house,
Would I get beyond the fright?

What would I say to an alien,
Who came to speak to me?
And wanted someone to ride with him,
Across the galaxy?

I've thought real hard about it,
And I think I'd say, *"Hey mister,*
If you want someone to go with you,
Why don't you take my sister?"

84

BUT WHAT IF.....

But what if.....
        I throw up and get sick,
        It bites me on the nose,
        My eyelids swell and stick,
        I fall and break my toes.
        My teeth all crack and chip,
        My hair gets stuck together,
        I try to walk, but trip,
        My skin gets tough as leather.

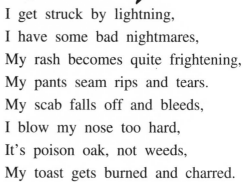

                I get struck by lightning,
                I have some bad nightmares,
                My rash becomes quite frightening,
                My pants seam rips and tears.
                My scab falls off and bleeds,
                I blow my nose too hard,
                It's poison oak, not weeds,
                My toast gets burned and charred.

I break your nicest vase,
I cough and sneeze all night,
I squash your eyeglass case,
My shoes are way too tight.
I act real mean and yucky,
I scare away my friends,
I seem to be unlucky,
My misfortune never ends......

Will you still love me?

BUBBLEMANIA

Bubbles, bubbles, bubbles,
Filling up the air,
Let's blow some more and then,
They'll be bubbles everywhere.

Billowy and soft ones,
Oozing all around,
Twist in funny shapes,
While sinking to the ground.

Little ones in clumps,
A floating bubble city,
Bump and pop in unison,
Like fireworks so pretty.

The colors of the rainbow,
You can very clearly see,
In each and every bubble,
As they float so high and free.

What are bubbles made of?
It's liquid in the jar,
But when you blow, they're stiff enough,
To journey off quite far.

For science I must study,
The bubble mystery,
I'll spend my summer watching them,
Just bubbles, fun, and me!

THAT'S NOT ME

Nobody likes a wiseguy,
Nobody likes a punk,
Nobody likes a bully,
Those kids are surely sunk.

So why do we sometimes act,
Like those who make a fuss?
Perhaps wiseguys, and bullies, and punks,
Are living in each of us.

IT'S PUZZLING

Jigsaw puzzles puzzle me,
I don't know why they make 'em,
It makes no sense, I must be dense,
I hate 'em, you can take 'em.

Why cut apart a pretty scene,
Into pieces all mixed up,
Then spend hours sorting them,
To get it all fixed up?

When Humpty Dumpty fell off the wall,
He was a sorry sight,
The project was too big for all,
They couldn't make him right.

I feel like that with puzzles,
The pieces never fit,
They look the same, oh what a shame,
It makes me want to quit.

I figured out a way to get
Around the puzzle's flaw,
I'll fix those bumps, smooth out the lumps,
Just let me have a saw!

PILL PROBLEM

You must be crazy,
My throat's too small,
That pill's as big
As a bowling ball.
It'll never fit,
I'll surely choke,
Is this your idea
Of a funny joke?
I'll swig some water,
The pill will melt,
It'll be the worst taste
I've ever felt.
So go away,
I'd rather be sick,
Or get some liquid medicine,
For me real quick.

THE MOST
INCREDIBLE
MACHINE

It can run,
It can jump,
It can bounce,
It can grow,
It's the most incredible
Machine I know.

It can see,
It can hear,
It can eat,
It can feel,
And if it gets damaged,
Itself it can heal.

It can bend,
It can twist,
It can stretch,
It can shrink,
Most incredible of all,
It really can think....

Say hello to your body!

91

so WHAT?

Who cares?

To care about something
Is to be alive.
If no one cared,
The world would be a sorry place.

What does it matter?

If you don't take pride in your work,
Everyone notices.
If you do take pride in your work,
Everyone notices, too.

What's the use?

If you try you might fail.
But you also might succeed.
If you give up,
You'll never know.

"JUST GET DRESSED"

What day is it?
What should I wear?
Rainy or sunny,
Is it cold out there?

I'm looking for socks,
Can't find a pair,
Now I'm in trouble,
No clean underwear.

This outfit's wrong,
The colors clash,
The missing pieces,
Must be in the wash.

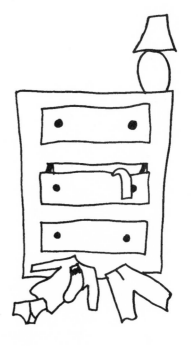

Don't know what else,
I can try to do,
I've nothing to wear,
I swear, it's true.

Aha, here they are,
My favorite clothes,
I'm ready now,
Yes! Here goes -

"Are you wearing that again?
Go back and change."

93

ALPHABETICALLY SPEAKING

I've learned to print so nice,
I practice quite a lot,
It's simple once you learn it,
But you want to know what?

I don't understand,
Why printing's not enough,
There's so many different alphabets,
It makes it very tough.

Plain, old **BLOCK** letters,
Are easy on the eyes,

But reading SHADOW letters,
Takes me quite a few tries.

I can't read BUBBLE letters,
For you know what they do?
They're soft and glob around the page,
And stick together, too.

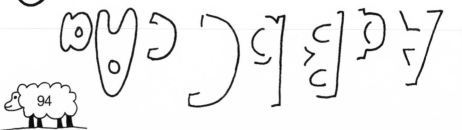

Aa Bb Cc

𝔒𝔩𝔡 𝔢𝔫𝔤𝔩𝔦𝔰𝔥 isn't better,
I won't read it, I refuse,
The letters are so complicated,
Too many curlicues.

THIS FANCY TYPE of printing,
Looks very weird at best,
Some letters are okay alone,
But I can't follow the rest.

The most horrible is *script*,
I still don't get it yet,
The words all look like scribbles,
Worst letters that I've met.

To alphabet inventors,
I'll give this little tip,
If you were in my class at school,
You'd all fail penmanship!

LAST MINUTE PRAYER

I guess I should have studied,
I'll try to do my best,
I didn't think it'd be this hard,
Please help me pass this test.

Number one's correct,
I'm not so sure of two,
There's lots of blanks
    throughout the page,
I've only answered a few.

Why am I so stupid?
Why am I so dumb?
I should have studied
    when I had the time,
It might have helped me some.

If I do well I promise,
I'll never be a dunce,
I'll study every waking hour,
Just help me pass this once!

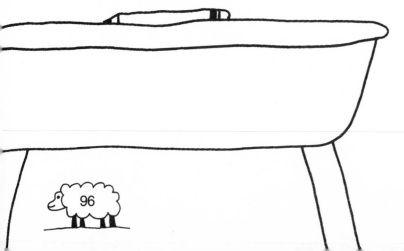

96

A NOT-SO-FRIGHTENING THOUGHT

What are nightmares?
They are the leftover
Fears and worries
In our lives
That are trying to escape.

SUPERHEROES

It's great to start my day,
It's sticky and so sweet,
And best of all it doesn't matter,
What we have to eat.

It covers up my pancakes,
My bacon and french toast,
It's even good with mushy eggs,
I like this food the most.

It tastes so good on waffles,
Ham and sausage, too,
I recommend it highly,
For me, as well as you.

And if my Mom would let me,
I'd pour it on cereal,
It wouldn't just be for breakfast,
But each and every meal.

I'm talking about syrup,
As if you didn't know,
It makes all food taste good to me,
And probably makes me grow.

There is another food,
Like syrup, it saves the day,
When vegetables and meat and stuff,
Seem to get in my way.

When it's time for dinner,
When we all sit down to sup,
If I don't like what's being served,
I smother it with ketchup!

A NEW ORDER

Do this, do that,
The orders are never-ending,
I look as if I'm listening, but in truth
I'm really pretending.

Come here, go there,
It's confusing I do find,
Why don't they stop and think before
They try to make up their mind?

Listen up, pay attention,
I'm talking to you for real,
If someone treated YOU this way,
How do you think *you'd* feel?

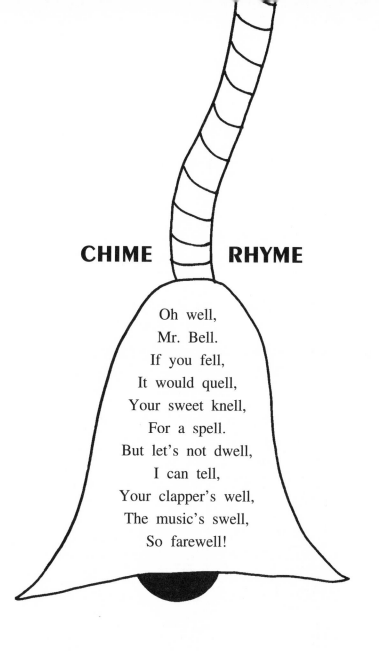

CHIME RHYME

Oh well,
Mr. Bell.
If you fell,
It would quell,
Your sweet knell,
For a spell.
But let's not dwell,
I can tell,
Your clapper's well,
The music's swell,
So farewell!

MY FAVORITE SUBJECTS

My two favorite subjects in school,
Are awesome and radically cool,
They're recess and lunch,
I like them a bunch,
You can see that I'm nobody's fool.

The only mistake that they made,
If they'd like free advice and some aid,
Is these subjects are so,
Important, you know,
That they ought to be given a grade!

Math	C-	~~~~
Language	D	~~~~
Science	B-	~~~~
Spelling	D-	~~~~
Lunch	A+	~~~~
Recess	A+	~~~~

SULKING

I'm so mad
I want to spit,
This is not
The end of it.
I was right,
And they were wrong,
I won't stay here
For very long.
No, I'll show them,
I'll make them cry,
I'll stay in here
Until I die.
They'll be sorry,
Wait and see,
They'll wish they hadn't
Punished me.
So even if
I'm here all night,
I'll prove my point -

I WAS RIGHT!

I'VE FALLEN AND I CAN'T GET UP!

Strap on the wheels,
This looks like fun,
I'd like to skate,
Like everyone.

Hurry up,
I want to go,
I'm ready now,
Okay....yikes....whoa!

Let me hold on,
How could I have known?
That both of my feet,
Have minds of their own.

I can't get started,
Or move at all,
As soon as I roll,
I immediately fall.

Can't pick up my feet,
Need to shuffle around,
And pray my backside,
Doesn't visit the ground.

For if it does,
I don't have the skill,
To get up with feet,
That won't stay still.

There's no way to stop,
When you pick up speed,
You just roll forever,
So please take heed:

I don't think that this
Was meant to be,
Most certainly not,
For someone like me.

For if God had wanted us
To *SKATE* down the street,
He'd have given us wheels,
Instead of our feet!

105

A TAXING EXPERIENCE

Here's the big moment,
The first time, you see,
I'm using allowance,
To buy something for me.

I pick out my toy,
I wait on the line,
I know what the price is,
It's one ninety-nine.

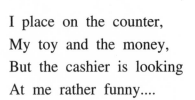

I have my two dollars,
Right in my hand,
So far it's all going,
Just as I planned.

I smooth out the money,
The closer I get,
What do I say?
Is it my turn yet?

I place on the counter,
My toy and the money,
But the cashier is looking
At me rather funny....

What do you mean, $1.99 plus **TAX?**
What's *TAX?*

BEST FRIEND

It's someone to rely on,
And have secrets that you share,
To play, talk, and pretend with,
And horse around and dare.

It's someone who sticks by you,
Even if it's trouble you're in,
Who tells you when you're acting wrong,
And likes to play to win.

It's someone who you care for,
Who returns that care with fun,
A best friend is a precious thing,
We all need at least one.

DO I HAFTA?

I don't wanna get up,
Do I hafta get up?
Please let me sleep some more,
Every day it's the same,
For this, school's to blame,
It's something I cannot ignore.

I don't wanna get dressed,
Do I hafta get dressed?
Please first let me eat some food,
That way when I'm done,
To my bedroom I'll run,
Can't you see that I'm in a bad mood?

I don't wanna go to school,
Do I hafta go to school?
Please let me stay home and play,
What d'ya mean, I'm confused?
You say you've good news?
ALL RIGHT! IT'S SATURDAY!!

LEAVE THEM ALONE

Why do leaves
Fall off of trees?
It makes me wonder so,
How nice it'd look,
When winter winds shook,
Leafy branches full of snow.

It seems so mean,
They're naked and clean,
I wish they could stay dressed,
For when the trees,
Are full of leaves,
That's when I like them the best.

109

WALK A MILE
IN MY SHOES

Now they've really done it,
They've gotten me upset,
Why do they talk so strangely with
These phrases I don't get?

    "I'm all ears" sounds odd to me,
    As well as **"suit youself,"**
    And how can people **"count on me,"**
    When I can't count myself?

"Mind your P's and Q's" is weird,
So is **"cream of the crop,"**
"There's more than one way to skin a cat,"
Has definitely got to stop.

"More fun than a barrel of monkeys,"
A crowded place to be,
And **"that's the way the cookie crumbles,"**
So messy, obviously!

"Don't look a gift horse in the mouth,"
Makes no sense, none at all,
And what does it mean not to **"spill the beans?"**
Whose beans and where will they fall?

I'd **"face the music"** if I knew,
Which way the music went,
I'd also **"bite the bullet,"**
If I knew just what that meant.

Trying to **"shoot fish in a barrel,"**
"Fits me to a tee,"
I'd **"wait until the cows come home,"**
But no cows live with me.

"It's not my cup of tea" is said,
But there's no tea around,
And how did **"curiosity kill the cat?"**
More confusion I've never found.

How about...

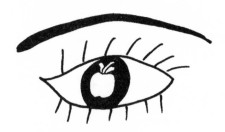

"You're the apple of my eye,"
The image seems so ghoulish,
And what do they mean when they say that I
Am **"penny wise, pound foolish?"**

Can you **"stick your foot in your mouth?"**
Seems difficult to me,
But if **"your eyes are bigger than your stomach,"**
It must be easy to see.

"Life's a bowl of cherries" yet
There is no fruit nearby,
And **"if the shoe fits wear it,"** but
Whose shoes am I to try?

These English language people,
Must be a bunch of rookies,
And if I knew what all this meant,
I'd probably **"toss my cookies!"**

TIME TO GO

I just got started,
And it's time to go,
Can't leave now,
I'll have you know.

This game is much too
Interesting,
Don't make me go
And leave everything.

Just one more turn,
Then I'll be done,
If I leave now,
Won't know if I won.

Why do you always
Do this to me?
It makes me angry,
Can't you see?

Just as I get
Involved in a game,
The voice I hear,
Is always the same:

"C'mon, it's time to go!"

113

"CLEAN UP YOUR ROOM"

It's not all junk,
It's not all clutter,
But she threatens to throw it
All in the gutter.

Everything's special,
Know what I mean?
Reminders of all that
I've done and seen.

It's not very neat,
This I'll admit,
But I can still find
A place to sit.

Things on the desk,
Bed, dresser, and floor,
If you open the closet,
You'll find much more.

114

She says she always
Enters with dread,
And can't even find
A path to my bed.

With that attitude
She shouldn't come inside,
This is my favorite place,
To think, play, and hide.

But she barges past,
And yells quite brash,
*"It's going to all
Go out with the trash!"*

To her it's a mess,
To be cleared away,
She doesn't understand,
I like it this way.

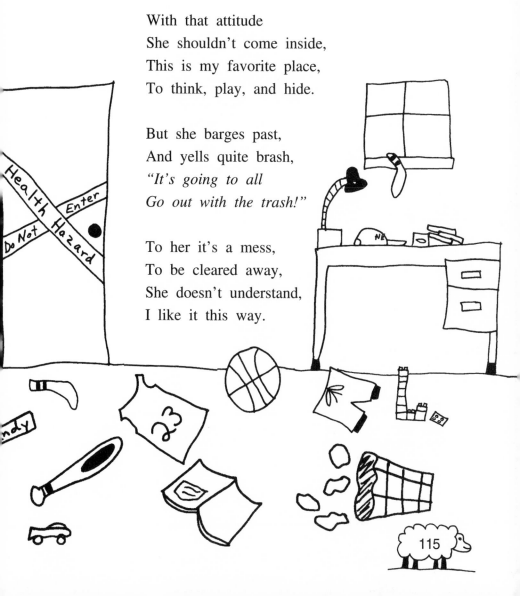

115

MATURITY

I'm supposed
To be mature.
But I'm not sure
what that means.
I try to act like them.
Be grownup.
But they tell me to
Do as they say,
Not as they do.
It doesn't make sense to me.

HAIR'S THE TRUTH
ABOUT BARBERS

I know he's called a barber, but
In this I'm much too wise,
He's actually a frustrated
Landscaper in disguise.

The scissors are so huge and fast,
It puts me right on edge,
He snips, and cuts, and chops, and shapes,
As if I'm some big hedge.

The itchy hair goes down my back,
I feel like such a wreck,
And then he takes the razor and
He weedwhacks down my neck.

The thing that really bothers me,
My hair, it keeps on growing,
And pretty soon I know that I
Will need another mowing!

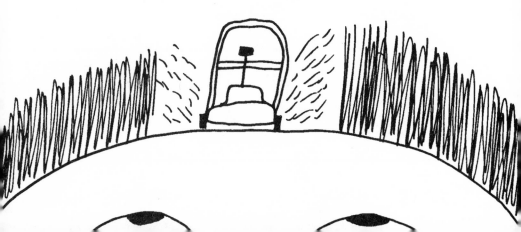

EXPLOSIONS
OF FUN

Can't wait,
Done yet?
Best snack
I ever et.

   Pop.

Crun-chy,
Salty, too,
And it's so darn
Good for you.

   Pop..........pop.

Starts small,
Needs heat,
Big explosions,
Funny treat.

   Pop.........pop......pop...pop.

Smells good,
Almost done,
Get the butter,
Start the fun!

Pop, pop, pop, pop, pop, pop, pop, pop, pop, pop,
pop, pop, pop, pop, pop, pop, pop, pop, pop, pop,
pop, pop, pop, pop, pop, pop, pop, pop, pop, pop,
pop, pop, pop, pop, pop, pop, pop, pop, pop, pop,
pop, pop, pop, pop, pop, pop, pop, pop, pop, pop,
pop..pop....pop.....pop......pop..............pop.....................pop!!

AT THE ZOO

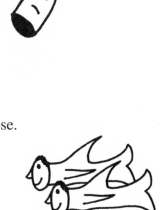

Ever wonder why,
It is we cannot fly?
Or why we have no trunk,
Nor smell bad like a skunk?
And sometimes don't you wish,
You could swim just like a fish?
And wouldn't it be a laugh,
To have a long neck like a giraffe?
Or jump so high and true,
Like the bouncy kangaroo?
I think it'd be real swell,
To have a turtle's shell.
I wonder if I'd hear,
With antlers like reindeer.
Or like the seal, I suppose,
Things could balance on my nose.
Sometimes I wish with a smile,
To trade places for a while,
And see how it would be,
To be an animal instead of me.
I think these thoughts anew,
Every time I visit the zoo!

A COURAGEOUS THOUGHT

What is courage?
It is what makes us
Stand tall
When we really want
To run and hide.

PIT STOP

Hurry up, oh hurry up,
I need to go real bad,
Please find a bathroom, stop the car,
I'll be so very glad.

I should have gone before we left,
But I didn't have to go,
It's been so long since we last stopped,
I need a bathroom so!

Please stop the car along the road,
No longer can I wait,
I'll jump right out, relieve myself,
Ooops!.......guess it's a little too late......

AUX   VCR   CABLE   TV

REMOTE CONTROL

This program is so boring.....................................click,
Oh, this one's stupid, too...click,
I don't want to watch the news at all....................click,
Good programs are too few..........................click..click.
This program is too scary.....................................click,
Oooh, too much blood and gore...........................click,
Nah, don't want to watch a cooking show...........click,
There isn't too much more.........................click..click.
This comedy's too silly...click,
This movie's black and white................................click,
This game show makes no sense to me................click,
What should I watch tonight?.....................click..click.
Well, I don't like to admit it................................click,
It's very hard for me..click,
My folks were right when they both said.............click,
There's nothing on TV...............................click..click.
I've gone through all the channels......................click,
It's something that I knew.....................................click,
I need to turn the TV off.....................................click,
And find something else to do!.................click..**CLICK!**

123

WHICH WAY DO THEY GO?

There are some very special words,
That seem to be a game,
Spell them back or forwards,
And they always stay the same.

I'd like to see if you agree,
Refer to the words below,
They look the same all turned around,
The *deed* is done like so:

My *Mom*, I like to call her *ma'am*,
My *Pop* is really *Dad*,
I have a *pup* that I named *Bob*,
Aha, he *sees* I'm glad.

I'm being on the *level*,
My cat, *Otto*, sleeps 'til *noon*,
He acts like he has *radar* ears,
And likes to *toot* at the moon.

Took my *race car* for a fast drive,
Put my *kayak* in the lake,
Watched a *tot* as she was napping,
Not a *peep did* she ever make.

124

A **tenet** that I have is
An idea or a belief,
The **civic** center's fun to go
To play in for relief.

And then there was the Garden,
Where **Eve** first met her date,
"Madam, I'm Adam" he said to her,
I think you know their fate.

The best one of the bunch, however,
Is not a word at all,
It is a sentence Napolean said,
A long time after his fall.

WOW

Napolean was a great ruler,
Exiled to an island with dread,
On Elba he spent many days,
Where alone he finally said:

"Able was I ere I saw Elba."

PILLOW TALK

Fluffy, light,
So snuggly at night,
But it's best used,
For a pillow fight.

Bop 'em hard,
Smack 'em strong,
Used as a shield,
You can't go wrong.

When my head hurts,
What feels the best,
Is to put my pillow,
On my forehead and rest.

And when it's hot,
What can you do?
Turn your pillow over,
Nice and cool for you.

Of all the things,
I can count on for sure,
My pillow makes me,
Feel most secure.

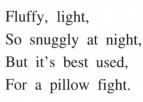

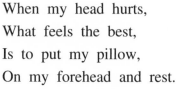

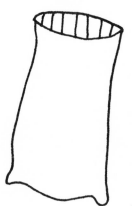

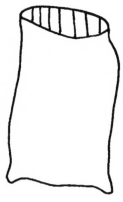

WHAT
ARE PRIVILEGES?

They're something invented by parents,
Just so they can take them away,
When you don't do everything they ask,
Or say what they want you to say.

Teachers also get into the act,
They look for a chance to remove,
Any privilege they set up if you disobey,
What are they trying to prove?

Getting a privilege is too much hard work,
They're much too easy to lose,
I'd rather have nothing special to do,
And behave however I choose!

Echo   Echo

Echo   Echo

THE ECHO GAME

I like to play the echo game,
I like to play the echo game,
Don't you?
Don't you?
It's easy to annoy someone,
It's easy to annoy someone,
That's true.
That's true.

And when you play the echo game,
And when you play the echo game,
Watch out.
Watch out.
The other guy will get so mad,
The other guy will get so mad,
He'll shout.
He'll shout.

E cho   Echo

ɘɥɔƎ   oɥɔƎ

When all he really has to do,
When all he really has to do,
To win.
To win.
Is stay as silent as he can,
Is stay as silent as he can,
And grin.
And grin.

But the bestest way I know to beat,
But the bestest way I know to beat,
Your foe.
Your foe.
Is smack him hard and make HIM yell,
Is smack him hard and make HIM yell,
Then echo.
Then echo.

MR. SUN

C'mon, Mr. Sun,
Come out and play,
Shove away those clouds,
It's a beautiful day.

Please don't be scared,
I know you're shy,
Come out from hiding,
And light up the sky.

We need a friend,
Who's fuzzy and warm,
To wake up the day,
Our morning alarm.

So don't be upset,
If it should rain,
Put on your best smile,
And come out again!

BUS RIDE

Lots of kids and
Deafening noise,
Girls with girls and
Boys with boys.
Jumping up and
Horsing around,
Can't sit still
Without a sound.

Opening windows and
Yelling outside,
Throwing things around,
Where is their pride?
Why are they always
Making a fuss?
What happens to kids
When they ride on the bus?

The bumpiest ride,
The wheels feel square,
But I wish it was longer,
Until we were there.
'Cause unlike the car,
You've the greatest view,
You can fool around,
And not get caught, too!

LIFE IS FRAGILE

Cuts and bruises, cuts and bruises,
Are something I'd gladly do without,
Bumps and scrapes, bumps and scrapes,
I guess that's what life is all about.

Don't want to fall, don't want to get hurt,
I want to do it all right,
But accidents happen, some can't be prevented,
They're not always a pretty sight.

We learn from mistakes, so maybe it's good,
That life roughs us up a bit,
It makes us appreciate health is a gift,
And we shouldn't go fooling with it.

So next time you're hurt, remember these words,
And see what a difference they make,
Have respect for your wounds as reminders, of course,
How quickly we all can break.

4 SIMPLE MATH ?

One.1
Single, solo, unit.

Two..2,2
Double, duet, duad.

Three...3,3,3
Triple, trio, triad, triangle.

Four....4,4,4,4
Quadruple, quartet, tetrad, quadrilateral, tetrahedron.

Five.....5,5,5,5,5
Quintuple, quintet, pentad, pentagon, pentahedron.

Six......6,6,6,6,6,6
Sextuple, sextet, hexad, hexagon, hexahedron.

Seven.......7,7,7,7,7,7,7
Septuple, septet, heptad, heptagon, heptahedron.

Eight........8,8,8,8,8,8,8,8
Octuple, octet, octad, octagon, octahedron.

Nine.........9,9,9,9,9,9,9,9,9
Noncuple, nonet, ennead, nonagon, enneahedron.

Ten..........10,10,10,10,10,10,10,10,10,10
Decuple, decet, decade, decagon, decahedron.

Whew.

Whoever said counting from one to ten was easy?

DOG LOVER

I love dogs,
I think they're great,
They're not a pet,
That you can hate.

They're not like cats,
Who never care,
Dogs show their love,
They're always there.

They somehow know,
When you are sad,
And cheer you up,
They're always glad.

They'll play forever,
And never get bored,
They want to please,
To get a reward.

Dogs can work,
Do things like that,
Who's ever seen,
A seeing eye cat?

Dogs protect you,
From all harm,
Better than that,
They're soft and warm.

So through it all,
You can depend,
Upon your dog,
To be your friend.

135

CAT LOVER

I love cats,
I think they're great,
They're not a pet,
That you can hate.

They're not like dogs,
Who sniff and drool,
Cats never do that,
It isn't cool.

You never need,
To walk a cat,
They use litterboxes,
And that's that.

Cats wash themselves,
And stay real clean,
They purr a lot,
See what I mean?

They like to play,
With a string or mouse,
Or chase you all
Around the house.

And when you need,
To feel warm and snug,
They curl in your lap,
Like a big, cat hug.

So through it all,
You can depend,
Upon your cat,
To be your friend.

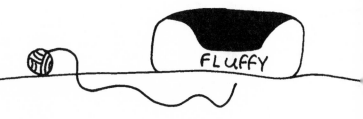

137

IT'S NOT A TOYBOX

Little bottles, little boxes,
Little pills all neat inside,
Doors that click and pop right open,
Or the kind that gently slide.

Little clippers, little scissors,
Little tubes of strange ointments,
It's full of things I'd like to play with,
Narrow shelves and many scents.

But I know I shouldn't do it,
All those things just might hurt me,
Medicines are poisons when
They're not used like they ought to be.

So listen to me, it's no joke,
It's dangerous at best,
To live a long and healthy life,
Don't play in the medicine chest!

FRECKLES

Why do people have them?
What purpose do they serve?
And why do folks make fun of them?
They surely have their nerve.

Some people have a few spots,
Across their cheeks and nose,
Others are all sprinkled,
From their heads down to their toes.

The summer sun is strong,
And makes them dark and clear,
By wintertime, however,
Mine always disappear.

So when I think about it,
The answer that I seek,
Is freckles are a special way,
To make us each unique.

CELEBRATION OF LIFE

Happy, happy, I'm so happy,
What a great day to be alive,
Nothing at all can bother me,
Why don't you just slip me five?

Pretty soon the fun will start,
I can't wait for it to begin,
I have a funny feeling that
Whatever game I play I'll win.

All my friends will play with me,
I'll be the star throughout the day,
They'll get me lots of toys and things,
Wouldn't have it any other way.

There's nothing better in the world,
That anyone can do or say,
It's the best event I know of,
Celebrating my BIRTHDAY!

NOT ON
THE SAME
WAVELENGTH

I know AM is morning,
And PM's after lunch,
But looking at the radio,
I haven't got a hunch -

AM's on the dial,
But I can't find PM,
And will someone please tell me,
What part of the day's FM?

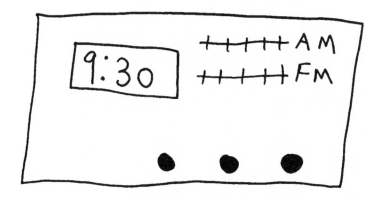

PRETZELFUN

Bite off the bottom, you've got an "8,"
Then chomp off one loop and you have a "D,"
Munch the straight side off of that letter,
Then you wind up with a "U" or "C."

Take another, bite off the bottom,
Gobble the two straight lines real fast,
What you're left with after this snacking,
Is a pretty "3" at last.

Let's do it again with another pretzel,
Eat the bottom, got any clue?
Snap off one curvy section carefully,
Now you have "p," "b," "d," or "q."

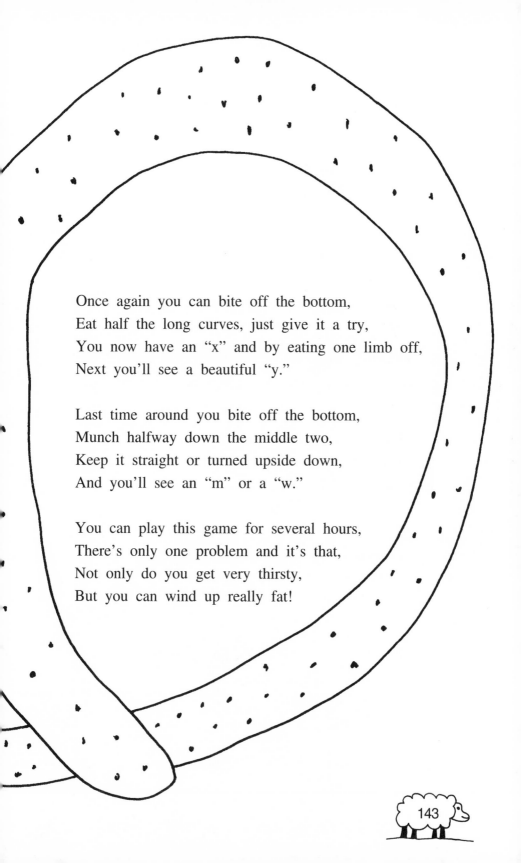

Once again you can bite off the bottom,
Eat half the long curves, just give it a try,
You now have an "x" and by eating one limb off,
Next you'll see a beautiful "y."

Last time around you bite off the bottom,
Munch halfway down the middle two,
Keep it straight or turned upside down,
And you'll see an "m" or a "w."

You can play this game for several hours,
There's only one problem and it's that,
Not only do you get very thirsty,
But you can wind up really fat!

SOUND EFFECTS

Nah, nah, nah, nah, nah,

I'm an air guitar,

Errrr, Arrrr, Urrrr, vroooOM,

I shift my racing car.

Nyaaaaaaaaaaaaaaaaaaaaaah,

The police are here,

wOO - woo, WOO - woo, WOO - woo,

An ambulance is near.

Eeeeeeeeeeeeeeuuuuuuw - KABOOM!!

An exploding bomb,

Eh-eh-eh-eh-eh-eh-eh,

Machine guns disrupt the calm.

HONK - shoo, HONK - shoo, HONK - shoo,

I'm snoring like my Dad,

Portable sound effects,

The best fun that I've had.

TRUSTY TONGUE

Sometimes things are salty,
Sometimes things are sweet,
But through it all your tongue will
Say hello to what you eat.

When things are very sour,
You pucker up your face,
Your tongue stays put, but helps you out,
It really knows its place.

If medicine is bitter,
Or you need to take a pill,
Your tongue will gag so Mom will know,
It isn't just your will.

And when you're very angry,
At someone who's a lout,
Your tongue knows what it has to do,
It sticks itself way out........

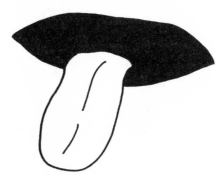

THE LIBRARY

Books, books, books,
They're all around,
They go from the ceiling,
Down to the ground.

Around the room,
On every wall,
Millions of books,
Look at them all!

And it's the neatest thing,
Without a doubt,
With one little card,
You can take them all out!

I FEEL A POEM
COMING ON

I cannot stop it,
Here it is,
It's like a sneeze,
Or soda fizz.
An idea pops
Into my head,
I cannot rest,
Until it's said.
I have to stop,
Get paper, pen,
Collect my thoughts
Real quick, and then....
The words all spill,
Onto the page,
Act out the thought,
Like on a stage.
And when it's done,
I can sit back,
For I survived,
A poem attack!

LOVE GROWS

Everybody gets the nasties,
Everybody gets real mean,
Everybody has their rotten days,
It's something everybody's seen.

Everybody has their good days,
Everybody can be kind,
Everybody has a soft spot,
It's something everybody finds.

It's easy to be with someone,
When they're having a good, sweet day,
It's pleasant and makes you feel good,
To be around someone this way.

But the harder task, it's true,
Is to be with a nasty soul,
The meanness gets contagious,
And nastiness takes its toll.

It's much more rewarding, however,
And a much more challenging test,
To stay with a grumpy person,
And try to bring out their best.

So don't ever get discouraged,
By folks full of gloom and despair,
For kindness will always grow on them,
If you just give it time and care.

149

FAREWELL

This is it,
This is the end,
Don't want to do it,
Think I'll cry.
You've listened to me,
Been my friend,
But now I have
To say good-bye.
Maybe someday,
When we're older,
We will meet,
And say hello.
But for now,
Try to remember,
I will always,
Love you so.....

Bye.

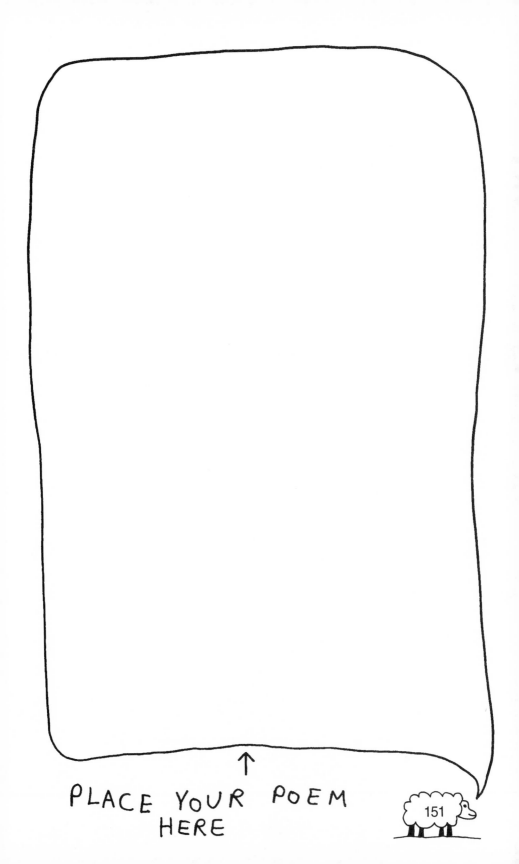

PLACE YOUR POEM
HERE

↑

151

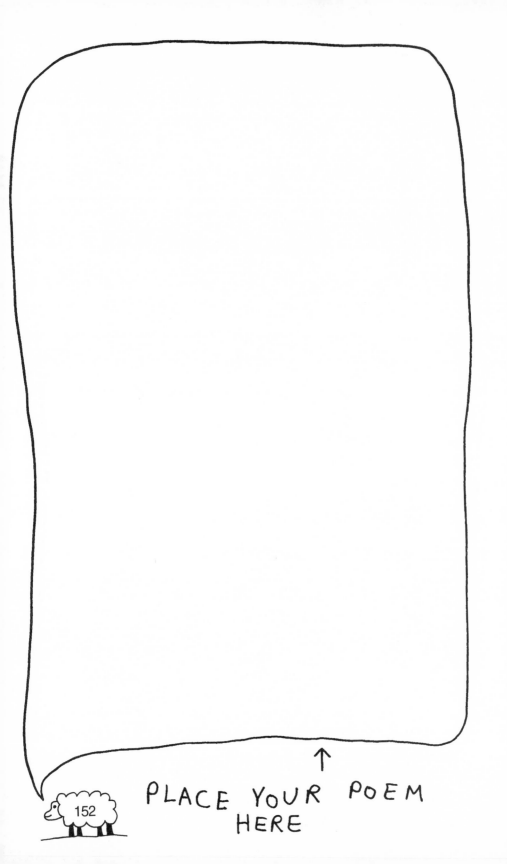

↑
PLACE YOUR POEM
HERE

152

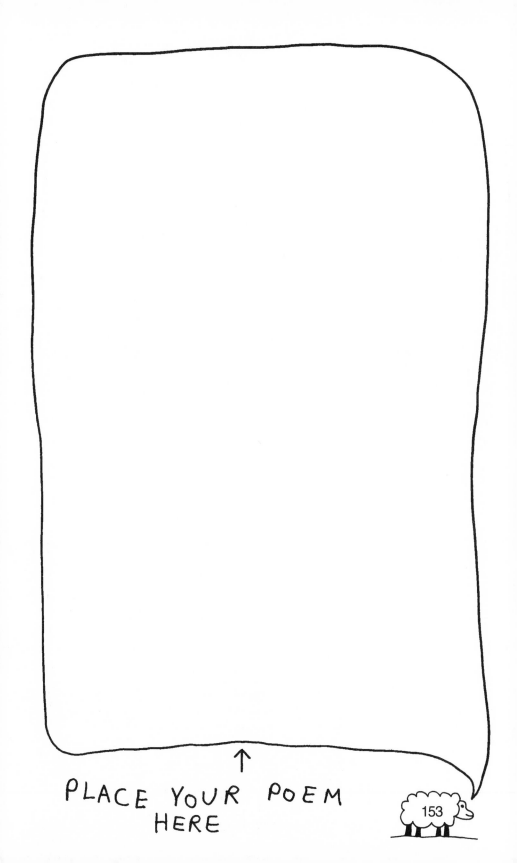

PLACE YOUR POEM
HERE

153

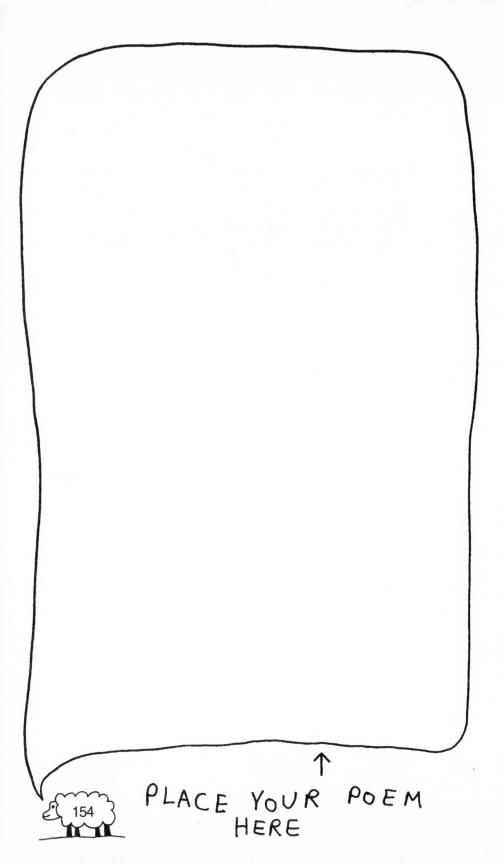

PLACE YOUR POEM HERE

↑

154

ACKNOWLEDGEMENTS

How can I express the joy I feel that God has enabled me to find something to do with my life that I so thoroughly enjoy? Writing for and speaking to children have opened my eyes to the reality that we have such a large responsibility and yet such a short time to try to improve the world we live in as we pass through it. We are transient. The world remains. The only things that endure are the values we pass along from generation to generation. Our most important task and the one with the most long-lasting consequences is equipping our children with enough love, sensitivity, caring, and forgiveness so that they can face this often difficult world and perhaps change it for the better also.

Once again, this book would not exist if it were not for my loving husband Doug and my wonderfully humorous and creative sons Luke, Jon, and Tom. They are the lifeblood of these poems. The boys also spent countless hours designing the covers and creating the illustrations. Doug put up with countless hours of neglect, but his support never waivered, nor did his humor. And they all put up with countless hours of me in the midst of computer burnout, which is not always a pretty sight.

The support of family and friends cheering and coaching me along made this effort all worthwhile. Your constant feedback via calls and letters made me sure that this is the right direction for me and these are the messages people want to hear.

And many, many thanks to Pam Shapiro and her artistic talents. Thanks for helping me grow. Thanks for teaching me to break out of the box. Thanks for the hours of page layout suggestions (you _are_ always right), tea, talk, and friendship. And thanks to Sean, Kelsey, and Allison for sharing your Mom with me. I know I took her away from important time with you.

And now I've used my one little voice enough and I must say good-bye. My work is finished - or has it just begun?

INDEX

Additional Comments:

Mail this order form and your check or money order to
(allow 4-6 weeks for delivery):

   Hereami Publishing, P.O. Box 261 Butler, NJ 07405-0261

If you have any questions, please call (973) 838-2685 or fax (973) 492-1525.

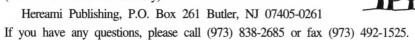

Additional Comments:

Mail this order form and your check or money order to
(allow 4-6 weeks for delivery):

   Hereami Publishing, P.O. Box 261 Butler, NJ 07405-0261

If you have any questions, please call (973) 838-2685 or fax (973) 492-1525.

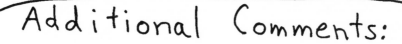

TO ORDER ADDITIONAL COPIES OF THE BOOKS:

a.) **THE GIANT & THE MOUSE:** ____ books @ $ 9.95 per book = $ _____

b.) **ONE LITTLE VOICE:** ____ books @ $ 9.95 per book = $ _____

c.) NJ residents add 6% sales tax = $ _____

d.) Add $2.00 shipping and handling for the first book
and $ .50 for each additional book = $ _____

Enclosed please find my check or money order (no cash or CODs) payable to Hereami Publishing, in the amount of (total lines a., b., c. & d.) $ _____.

The books should be shipped to:

Name _____

Address _____

City _____ State ____ Zip _____

Mail this order form and your check or money order to (allow 4-6 weeks for delivery):
Hereami Publishing, P.O. Box 261 Butler, NJ 07405-0261
If you have any questions, please call (973) 838-2685 or fax (973) 492-1525.

TO ORDER ADDITIONAL COPIES OF THE BOOKS:

a.) **THE GIANT & THE MOUSE:** ____ books @ $ 9.95 per book = $ _____

b.) **ONE LITTLE VOICE:** ____ books @ $ 9.95 per book = $ _____

c.) NJ residents add 6% sales tax = $ _____

d.) Add $2.00 shipping and handling for the first book
and $ .50 for each additional book = $ _____

Enclosed please find my check or money order (no cash or CODs) payable to Hereami Publishing, in the amount of (total lines a., b., c. & d.) $ _____.

The books should be shipped to:

Name _____

Address _____

City _____ State ____ Zip _____

Mail this order form and your check or money order to (allow 4-6 weeks for delivery):
Hereami Publishing, P.O. Box 261 Butler, NJ 07405-0261
If you have any questions, please call (973) 838-2685 or fax (973) 492-1525.

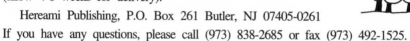

Additional Comments:

Mail this order form and your check or money order to
(allow 4-6 weeks for delivery):

    Hereami Publishing, P.O. Box 261 Butler, NJ 07405-0261

If you have any questions, please call (973) 838-2685 or fax (973) 492-1525.

Additional Comments:

Mail this order form and your check or money order to
(allow 4-6 weeks for delivery):

    Hereami Publishing, P.O. Box 261 Butler, NJ 07405-0261

If you have any questions, please call (973) 838-2685 or fax (973)

TO ORDER ADDITIONAL COPIES OF THE BOOKS:

a.) **THE GIANT & THE MOUSE:** ____ books @ $ 9.95 per book = $ _____

b.) **ONE LITTLE VOICE:** ____ books @ $ 9.95 per book = $ _____

c.) NJ residents add 6% sales tax = $ _____

d.) Add $2.00 shipping and handling for the first book
   and $ .50 for each additional book = $ _____

Enclosed please find my check or money order (no cash or CODs) payable to Hereami Publishing, in the amount of (total lines a., b., c. & d.) $ _____.

The books should be shipped to:

Name _____

Address _____

City _____ State _____ Zip _____

Mail this order form and your check or money order to (allow 4-6 weeks for delivery):
Hereami Publishing, P.O. Box 261 Butler, NJ 07405-0261
If you have any questions, please call (973) 838-2685 or fax (973) 492-1525.

TO ORDER ADDITIONAL COPIES OF THE BOOKS:

a.) **THE GIANT & THE MOUSE:** ____ books @ $ 9.95 per book = $ _____

b.) **ONE LITTLE VOICE:** ____ books @ $ 9.95 per book = $ _____

c.) NJ residents add 6% sales tax = $ _____

d.) Add $2.00 shipping and handling for the first book
   and $ .50 for each additional book = $ _____

Enclosed please find my check or money order (no cash or CODs) payable to Hereami Publishing, in the amount of (total lines a., b., c. & d.) $ _____.

The books should be shipped to:

Name _____

Address _____

City _____ State _____ Zip _____

Mail this order form and your check or money order to (allow 4-6 weeks for delivery):
Hereami Publishing, P.O. Box 261 Butler, NJ 07405-0261
If you have any questions, please call (973) 838-2685 or fax (973) 492-1525.

Additional Comments:

Mail this order form and your check or money order to
(allow 4-6 weeks for delivery):

    Hereami Publishing, P.O. Box 261 Butler, NJ 07405-0261

If you have any questions, please call (973) 838-2685 or fax (973) 492-1525.

Additional Comments:

Mail this order form and your check or money order to
(allow 4-6 weeks for delivery):

    Hereami Publishing, P.O. Box 261 Butler, NJ 07405-0261

If you have any questions, please call (973) 838-2685 or fax (973)

TO ORDER ADDITIONAL COPIES OF THE BOOKS:

a.) **THE GIANT & THE MOUSE:** ____ books @ $ 9.95 per book = $ _____

b.) **ONE LITTLE VOICE:** ____ books @ $ 9.95 per book = $ _____

c.) NJ residents add 6% sales tax = $ _____

d.) Add $2.00 shipping and handling for the first book
and $ .50 for each additional book = $ _____

Enclosed please find my check or money order (no cash or CODs) payable to Hereami Publishing, in the amount of (total lines a., b., c. & d.) $ _____.

The books should be shipped to:

Name _____

Address _____

City _____ State ____ Zip _____

Mail this order form and your check or money order to (allow 4-6 weeks for delivery):
Hereami Publishing, P.O. Box 261 Butler, NJ 07405-0261

If you have any questions, please call (973) 838-2685 or fax (973) 492-1525.

TO ORDER ADDITIONAL COPIES OF THE BOOKS:

a.) **THE GIANT & THE MOUSE:** ____ books @ $ 9.95 per book = $ _____

b.) **ONE LITTLE VOICE:** ____ books @ $ 9.95 per book = $ _____

c.) NJ residents add 6% sales tax = $ _____

d.) Add $2.00 shipping and handling for the first book
and $ .50 for each additional book = $ _____

Enclosed please find my check or money order (no cash or CODs) payable to Hereami Publishing, in the amount of (total lines a., b., c. & d.) $ _____.

The books should be shipped to:

Name _____

Address _____

City _____ State ____ Zip _____

Mail this order form and your check or money order to (allow 4-6 weeks for delivery):
Hereami Publishing, P.O. Box 261 Butler, NJ 07405-0261

If you have any questions, please call (973) 838-2685 or fax (973) 492-1525.